Sec

The Human Factor

Security

The Human Factor

PAUL KEARNEY

IT Governance Publishing

Every possible effort has been made to ensure that the information contained in this book is accurate at the time of going to press, and the publishers and the author cannot accept responsibility for any errors or omissions, however caused. No responsibility for loss or damage occasioned to any person acting, or refraining from action, as a result of the material in this publication can be accepted by the publisher or the author.

While web addresses were accurate on the date of publication, the sites concerned may since have been redesigned, moved or closed. In the event that a link is broken, try using a search engine like Google to track the document down. Alternatively, searching on the title of the reference, or enclosing it in double quotes may produce a better result.

IT Governance Publishing
IT Governance Limited
Unit 3, Clive Court
Bartholomew's Walk
Cambridgeshire Business Park
Ely
Cambridgeshire
CB7 4EH
United Kingdom

www.itgovernance.co.uk

First published in the United Kingdom in 2010 by IT Governance Publishing.

ISBN 978-1-84928-063-1

FOREWORD

The security of information – corporate, commercial and personal – is under greater threat than ever before.

The reason is a simple one. We are all caught up in an 'arms race' between a guerrilla army of thieves, hackers and mischief-makers on one side, and an equally determined force of 'good guys' on the other. As more and more of our lives go online and digital, the stakes are getting higher and higher.

So who are the good guys manning the defences?

It's tempting to focus solely on security professionals. They are, after all, the people who have the best understanding of what's at stake, the techniques the opposition use to mount attacks, and how to defend the premises and IT systems at threat.

But this view would be simplistic. No matter how highly skilled they are, security professionals cannot hope to protect organisations by working on their own. Take IT security, for example. These days, you hear far less about cases where hackers have managed to gain access to organisation's IT systems and steal information, and for good reason. IT security teams have become very good at their jobs. But stories of people leaving laptops on trains, confidential documents on display in public places, and so on, abound.

As this pocket guide makes clear, to protect organisations as effectively as possible, you need to focus on three things: people, processes and technology. No matter how much you invest in security processes and technologies, it will be wasted if your employees don't understand the issues at stake, how they can help protect your organisation, and how to use the processes and technologies involved.

Ray Stanton

Executive Global Head of Business Continuity, Security and Governance, BT Global Services

PREFACE

It is often suggested that the people who work in organisations, are the cause of most information security problems. They write passwords on Post-it® Notes, leave laptops on trains, talk about sensitive subjects in public places, and so on. Why can't they just obey the policies?

The problem with this view is that it is simplistic. Yes, people do cause problems, but this is not usually deliberate. Take a close look at any incident, and, more often than not, you'll find someone who was honestly trying to do the best-possible job he or she could, but was poorly trained in the use of security tools and procedures, was torn by conflicting priorities, or simply had no idea his or her actions could cause a problem.

In reality, three things matter – people, processes and technology. If organisations are to keep the IT systems they own, and the information they hold, secure, they must address all three. Not as independent components, but as a mutually supporting combination.

This pocket guide looks at the challenges this can involve, the consequences of failing to meet them, and, most importantly, at the steps organisations can take to make themselves, and their information, more secure.

I hope you find it useful.

Paul Kearney

ABOUT THE AUTHOR

Paul Kearney is Chief Security Researcher in the Security Futures Practice, BT Innovate and Design.

He joined BT in 1997, having previously worked in the personal electronics and defence aerospace industries.

Paul has worked in information security research since 2001. A Certified Information System Security Professional (CISSP), and a Member of the Institute of Information Security Professionals (MInstISP), he was a co-author of the white paper, 'Human Vulnerabilities in Security Systems', published in 2007 by the Cyber Security Knowledge Transfer Network. This Network is one of a number of government-funded bodies set up to keep the UK at the forefront of the digital revolution, by creating and sharing expertise.

Paul gained his BSc and PhD in theoretical physics from the Universities of Liverpool and Durham, respectively. He is based at BT's Adastral Park Technology Centre, near Ipswich in Suffolk.

CONTENTS

INTRODUCTION

'People sometimes make mistakes and do things they aren't supposed to. After all, they're only human. Technology, media and telecommunications organisations should focus more on the human facet of security, specifically internal vulnerabilities.'

Deloitte, 2010[1]

Damage to reputation and brand image, loss of revenue and customer base, leakage of IPR and commercial information to competitors, fines and criminal prosecution, are among the consequences for organisations that suffer security breaches.

Advances in information technology multiply the potential magnitude of breaches, and the speed at which their consequences propagate. Simultaneously, cybercriminals have grown organised and professional, served by a black economy in stolen information and malware toolkits. Every enterprise needs to be aware of the risks it is exposed to, it must review and refresh its security measures continually, and be ever-vigilant in case of their failure.

In a way, this is nothing new. On the mediaeval battlefield, knights protected themselves with armour made from articulated metal plates, chain mail and padding. Each plate had its purpose and was shaped accordingly, but also had to connect flexibly with its neighbours. The elements of the armour collectively had to cover all the strategic areas of the body – the head, chest, arms, and so on – but still had to allow the knight to function as a fighting machine.

Any vulnerability would quickly be exploited by more lowly, less well-equipped, but more numerous, and more agile, opponents. The design of the armour was therefore inevitably a compromise, between maximising strength and completeness of

---

[1] '2010 TMT Global Security Study: Key findings', Deloitte, 2010, *www.deloitte.com/assets/Dcom-Global/Local%20Assets/Documents/T MT/2010_TMT_Global_Security_study.pdf.*

coverage on the one hand, to minimising the impact on ease of movement, vision and communication, on the other. Issues such as cost and display of wealth and position, also played big parts.

Like the knight of yore, the modern organisation relies for protection on the harmonious interaction of dissimilar elements, often grouped under the headings of 'people', 'processes' and 'technology'. An opponent looking to compromise the organisation's information security, will naturally take the easiest route, and this is often by manipulating people, or exploiting their errors. It is tempting to conclude, then, that people are 'bad for security', and that matters should be taken out of their hands through automation or rigid discipline. But this would be a mistake. On the whole, staff do not wilfully breach security – the ease with which attackers can exploit them, is often the result of poorly designed technology and processes, or lack of appropriate training.

Many security professionals (myself included) are technologists, and it is natural for us to regard users as a necessary evil, from whom the technology must be protected. The opposite view – that to err is human, but to muck things up thoroughly takes a computer – is equally widespread, and equally wrong. The real issue is not that one side is good and the other evil, but that hardware and humans have very different characteristics. Whereas computers will perform the same task reliably, day after day, regardless of whether the results make sense, people will make mistakes, interpret instructions differently depending on mood, and apply their common sense for good or ill. It is not surprising, then, that many of the most significant security problems arise at the interface between humans and technology.

The third element of an organisation is the process. If we liken an organisation to a computer system, then business processes are essentially the programs that dictate what it does. These programs 'execute' on two different types of hardware – people and IT – each of which has strengths and weaknesses. The automation of parts of a business process can bring predictability and efficiency, but requires it to be specified prescriptively, in fine detail. If security loopholes are missed by the process designer, the predictability of the IT system becomes a weakness that can be exploited by an attacker – a weakness that can be exploited repeatedly in just a short space of time.

People, on the other hand, can interpret instructions. This is simultaneously a strength and a weakness. A person can cope with instructions that are poorly worded, and adapt those they are given to the circumstances they actually face.

Furthermore, employees can (and do) spot problems and suspicious activity, apply common sense, and use their initiative to intervene, or call for assistance. Unfortunately, they will also adapt, or indeed ignore completely, correctly- and precisely-worded instructions, if they appear not to make sense on first reading, or are inconvenient. From an attacker's point of view, however, the significant thing about them is that they can be manipulated.

The focus of this pocket guide is on addressing human vulnerabilities – that is, weaknesses in an organisation's security due to the characteristics and behaviours of people. However, because the three organisational elements depend on each other, we also need to consider the effect that processes and technology have on people's contribution to security.

The approach I propose, and set out in this pocket guide, has three main principles:

- Enable people to make a positive contribution to security through awareness campaigns, education, motivation and empowerment.

- Design processes, incentives and security policies, to minimise conflicts of interest, and make it easy for people to behave securely.

- Design technical solutions with interfaces that are easy to use, and that provide users with intuitive models of their functionality.

In the first chapter, I will discuss some human qualities that can lead to weaknesses, from a security point of view, although many of these also have a positive side.

CHAPTER 1: CARELESSNESS

'Human error is overwhelmingly stated as the greatest {security} weakness this year (86%), followed by technology (a distant 63%) ... Unless robots replace the human workforce (unlikely in the lifetime of anyone reading this report), human error is an issue that companies will continue to deal with.'

Deloitte, 2009[2]

Let's look at some of the ways that human nature can contribute to security breaches, beginning with carelessness.

Barely a week goes by without a report of a laptop, or a USB stick containing sensitive information, being left on a train, or being stolen when left in plain view on the back seat of a car. Modern electronic equipment is highly portable, and can hold staggering amounts of data. Employees are actively encouraged to take advantage of this portability, to work on the move, and at home, so they can hardly be criticised when they do. We're not just talking about laptops either. It's easy to underestimate the volume and value of information stored on smart phones, and the other devices that are used in both our business and our personal lives.

In times gone by, people going to meetings would just pack their briefcase with the papers they needed on the day. Everything else got left behind. Now, we can take everything but the proverbial kitchen sink with us – all our correspondence on every topic, every report that's crossed our desk, and far more besides.

In some ways, it's an advantage. There's no chance of getting to a meeting only to discover you left the most critical document

---

[2] 'Protecting what matters – 6th Annual Global Security Survey', Deloitte, 2009,
www.deloitte.com/view/en_CZ/cz/industries/fsi/article/66b7bf2733101 210VgnVCM100000ba42f00aRCRD.htm.

behind. But in other ways, it's a big problem. By taking so much with you, you're putting so much more at risk.

In January 2008, for example, a laptop was stolen from a Royal Navy recruiting officer's car. It contained personal information about 600,000 people who had joined Britain's armed forces, or expressed an interest in doing so[3]. The problems this could have caused are clear. As the Secretary of State for Defence at the time said, not only were details of bank accounts revealed, but the home addresses (and thus lives) of soldiers, sailors and airmen.

Such incidents are commonplace. Also in 2008, a consultant working for the Home Office copied the details of thousands of criminals onto a memory stick – then lost it. Data about 84,000 criminals was put at risk[4]. In 2009, a council worker lost a memory stick containing the names and bank details of more than 1,000 housing-benefit recipients[5]. And in 2010, the American healthcare provider, Kaiser Permanente, reported that a device stolen from an employee's car had contained records relating to 15,000 patients[6].

The cost of responding to such incidents is huge – the Ponemon Institute says American companies spend an average of US\$204 for every customer record lost[7].

So what can we do to reduce the likelihood and consequences of an incident?

---

[3] 'MoD lost three unencrypted laptops', ZDNet UK, 22 January 2008, *http://news.zdnet.co.uk/security/0,1000000189,39292312,00.htm.*
[4] 'Firm "broke rules" over data loss', BBC News, 22 August 2008, *http://news.bbc.co.uk/1/hi/7575989.stm*.
[5] 'Lost council data stick contained bank details of 1,000 residents', dash.com, 2 March 2009,
www.24dash.com/news/Local_Government/2009-03-02-Lost-council-d ata-stick-contained-bank-details-of-1-000-residents.
[6] 'Kaiser Patient Data Stolen', KRCA.com, 12 January 2010, *www.kcra.com/news/22220329/detail.html*.
[7] 'Ponemon study shows the cost of a data breach continues to increase', PR Newswire, 25 January 2010,
www.prnewswire.com/news-releases/ponemon-study-shows-the-cost-of -a-data-breach-continues-to-increase-82585957.html.

The most obvious answer is to take only what you need with you. It's tempting to carry extra information on a 'just in case' basis, or because it's easier to download complete databases than extract specific details. Taking a back-up copy on a USB stick may seem like a sensible precaution, but that also doubles your chances that the data will go missing. This goes for paper copies too, and while a paper document carries less information than a PC, the information is exposed for all to see.

Remote access facilities are so much better than they were, and are so much easier to use. Furthermore, public hotspots are spreading, and Wi-Fi is even available on some trains. (Note, however, that 'free public Wi-Fi' is not always what it seems.)

This removes the need for people to carry so much data around with them. The principle is a simple one: data is far safer when it's kept on central servers that are properly secured and managed. So, the best option is for people to leave it there and access it remotely, as and when required.

But what about the data people really do have to carry around? For that, full-disk encryption of built-in hard disk drives, and the automatically-enforced encryption of USB drives, is highly recommended. It may sound complicated, but it isn't difficult – or expensive – to do. Hardware-based solutions that can secure entire disks to standards that far exceed most organisations' needs, are available for as little as £200. Software-based solutions that protect data, file by file, are cheaper still, at £50 or less a machine. This may sound a lot, when compared to the falling prices of computer hardware. You can get a powerful laptop PC for a few hundred pounds, for example. But remember, the data on a device can be worth far more than the device itself. In that context, encryption is a bargain.

Remember also that the data is valuable to you, as well as to any thief. If your only copy of the 300-page report you've been writing is on the laptop that has just gone missing, it could really spoil your day! So, back-up your important work, ideally every day, and keep the copy safe and well away from the original.

Finally, it pays to be vigilant. Do not leave valuable equipment and documents unattended, and in plain view. If you're travelling by car, lock your laptop in the boot, rather than leaving it in the seat where it can be seen. Remember, that in some foreign countries, industrial espionage is rife – and even state-sponsored – so locked hotel rooms cannot be considered secure. Also, be aware of who is around you while you are working. Can the sensitive information on your screen be seen by the man or woman in the seat behind? And be careful what you say on the phone in public places. Think of what the consequences would be if someone working for one of your fiercest competitors was sitting at the next table.

Top tips ...

Don't carry any more data with you than you have to.

Encrypt disks and other data storage devices.

Make a back-up – every day!

Don't leave equipment and documents unattended.

Beware of prying eyes.

CHAPTER 2: ACCIDENTAL DISCLOSURE

'All great work is preparing yourself for the accident to happen.'

Sidney Lumet

'Oops!... I did it again.'

Britney Spears

This brings me nicely to my next topic – the accidental disclosure of information.

Even the heads of security-conscious organisations accidentally disclose data they are trying to protect. In April 2009, for example, Britain's most senior anti-terrorist policeman got out of a car and walked into Downing Street clutching a pile of paperwork[8]. On top of the pile, a page marked 'secret' was clearly visible. It set out plans for smashing what was thought to be a terrorist cell in Manchester.

Unfortunately, the bystanders included media photographers, equipped with high-resolution cameras, telephoto lenses, and so on. The government acted quickly to prevent photographs being published, but by then the cat was out of the bag. To minimise the 'damage', the raid on premises in Manchester was hastily brought forward. The policeman who caused the problem resigned shortly afterwards, but he wasn't the first, or last, to expose confidential documents in, or around, Downing Street.

In May 2008, Caroline Flint, the housing minister at the time, revealed fears that house prices would fall by 10% or more that year, and that the market for new homes was collapsing[9].

---

[8] 'Terror blunder: Police chief Bob Quick under pressure to resign', *The Daily Telegraph*, 9 April 2009,
www.telegraph.co.uk/news/uknews/5128478/Terror-blunder-police-chief-Bob-Quick-under-pressure-to-resisn.html.
[9] 'Blundering minister exposes secret Government fears that house prices will fall by at best 5-10% this year', *The Daily Mail*, 13 May

In September 2009, Lord Mandleson, then Business Secretary, revealed an assessment of the Labour Party's performance in Government, and ideas for attacking opposition parties in the run up to the next election[10].

And that's just the tip of the problem. Every day, thousands – probably millions – of people can be found holding confidential conversations, and reading confidential documents, on trains, in airport lounges, and in other public places. It's all too easy to be drawn unwittingly into discussing confidential matters with strangers, or with colleagues, in a social context, just to make oneself, or one's job, sound interesting.

As one Tweeter commented recently, 'I can't believe how people read confidential documents on the train for the world to see. I learn so much'.

Be warned!

Top tips ...

Don't read confidential documents in public places.

Don't discuss confidential matters in public places.

If you have to take confidential documents out of the office, put them in an envelope, or, better still, a locked case.

2008,
www.dailymail.co.uk/news/article-566129/Blundering-minister-expose
s-secret-Government-fears-house-prices-set-fall-best-5-10-year.html.
[10] 'Lord Mandelson is latest to expose confidential paper in Downing Street', *The Times,* 22 September 2009,
www.timesonline.co.uk/tol/news/politics/article6843506.ece.

CHAPTER 3: PEOPLE ARE INTELLIGENT

'Intelligence is not to make no mistakes, but quickly to see how to make them good.'

Bertolt Brecht

Computers will follow instructions reliably, as long as they are consistent and unambiguous. Humans may not do what they are told, if they don't see the point, but they will try to make sense of unclear instructions, and can cope in situations where instructions don't apply.

Often, employees are faced with a choice between complying, by getting on with their job, and incurring delays and inconvenience, by complying with security policy. An example of this is a policy that requires staff to use only their own individual accounts in an environment such as a shop or a hospital, where many staff share the same terminals. Under pressure of time, or a desire to be helpful, the temptation is to allow a colleague to process a transaction during your session, rather than logging off and on again. Merely enforcing a policy, either by technical means, or by threat of punishment, can be counter-productive. Employees can become de-motivated and resentful if they are treated as a cog in the machine, or a wayward child. They may also identify the control measure with the policy, feeling that if they find a way around the control, they are not breaking the policy. Furthermore, if a specific policy is perceived as unnecessary, petty, bureaucratic, or just plain wrong, the whole issue of security becomes discredited.

The situation can be made worse by naive productivity incentives. If rewards are based on the number of jobs processed, staff will find ingenious ways round security measures that slow them down. Worse still, security will be seen as the enemy of real work, rather than an important contributor to the health of the enterprise.

Software, and other technology that is difficult to use and understand, can cause similar problems. If staff are to use their common sense and judgement in balancing security and productivity, for example, they need to have in their minds a model of how the technology works. This is not at a deep technical level, but at a level that allows them to understand the consequences of the things they do, and the decisions they make.

If security technology comes with a set of operating instructions that simply have to be followed, without justification or explanation, it's all too easy for people to miss out a step or two. If things still seem to work, and nothing bad happens, they will reach what seems like the obvious conclusion – 'clearly those steps don't really matter'. But suppose the missing steps were to do with encrypting sensitive data on CDs to be sent through the post. Missing them out will not matter the 99 times out of every 100 the envelope is delivered correctly, but the 100th occasion could result in substantial fines and loss of business for the company, and possibly dismissal for the employee.

The same goes for security and business processes. Processes that are hard for people to understand or use will result in mistakes and well-meant 'improvements' and knock holes in their security. In contrast, processes that are well-designed and well-explained will enable staff to employ their common sense and ingenuity constructively, as they encounter unusual cases not catered for in the instructions. You never know, they may even come up with some genuine improvements!

There are no quick fixes and generally-applicable answers here – managing, motivating and educating people is a complex business. The main message is that you should do all you can to 'close the loop', and strive continuously for improvement. Engage with your staff, find out their opinions, and, where possible, take them into account. Observe actual behaviours, and, where they deviate from desirable practices, try to understand why, and respond to the issues at stake. We will return to these issues later on.

Top tips ...

Security procedures work best when they are built in to the applications and processes people use, rather than added to them.

Make sure people understand why you are asking them to do things.

Check your procedures fit the way people really work.

Seek and act on feedback.

CHAPTER 4: AN ASIDE: PASSWORD POLICIES

Password policies provide an interesting case study in the design of security procedures. Some say their days are numbered – that biometrics, smart-cards, and other such technologies, will replace them – but for some considerable time to come, organisations will control who can access their networks and IT systems, using usernames and passwords.

To be effective in security terms, a password must be remembered by its owner, but to all intents and purposes be a random jumble of characters to anyone else.

Unfortunately, people often choose passwords that are easy to remember – and are almost as easy for others to guess.

In January 2010, an unknown hacker stole a list of 32 million passwords from RockYou, an American company that develops software for use on social networking sites. The list, which was posted briefly on a number of websites, provided an interesting glimpse of the passwords users actually choose.

According to a report in the *New York Times,* one out of five users left ' the digital equivalent of a key under the doormat', by choosing easily guessed passwords, like *'abc123', 'iloveyou', 'qwerty',* and even *'password'.* The most popular was *'123456'*[11].

Given the extent of most people's digital footprints these days, it's probable that many less popular passwords would have been easy for hackers and fraudsters to work out. People often use words associated with their lives as passwords – their place of birth, for example, or the names of children or pets – assuming strangers would not know these facts. The trouble is that such details are increasingly posted on social networking sites, and in other public locations. People also tend to use the same

---

[11] 'If your password is 123456, just make it hackme', *New York Times,* 20 January 2010, www.nytimes.com/2010/01/21/technology/21password.html.

password for everything, so that poor security on some recreational website, may result in a criminal getting access to your bank accounts, or your work e-mail.

Organisations that take security seriously, limit the choices people can make. They require passwords to include letters and numerals, uppercase as well as lowercase characters, special characters, such as %, < and *, and to exceed a minimum length. Furthermore, they require passwords to be changed regularly. While all this makes it more difficult for others to guess the password, it also makes it hellishly difficult to remember. And of course, you must not write it down!

The strength of a password is a function of length, complexity and randomness, among other parameters. It will make as full use of the keyboard as possible – including not just upper- and lowercase letters and numbers, but punctuation marks and symbols, where they are allowed. And it will be as long as possible – eight characters is often regarded as the bare minimum. But password strength and security are not the same thing. Strength makes the password difficult to guess, but may actually increase the probability of disclosure, if it forces you to write the passwords down, for example.

Whether or not writing down a list of passwords is a problem, depends on where the list is kept. My colleague, Bruce Schneier, BT's Chief Security Technology Officer, recommends that, if people are intent on keeping a list, they use a small piece of paper, and keep it where they would keep similarly valuable items – in their wallet or purse[12]. That way, they'll know as soon as they are lost or stolen, and will be able to take action accordingly.

A safer alternative is to use a utility like Norton Identity Safe, or an encrypted document on your PC, to hold log-in details for individual applications and websites, making sure the password that opens your electronic 'safe' is 'strong'.

---

[12] 'Write down your password', Schneier on Security, 17 June 2005, *www.schneier.com/blog/archives/2005/06/write_down_your.html.*

An alternative strategy, recommended by Sarah Scalet, Senior Editor for *CSO Magazine,* in December 2009, is not to try and remember individual passwords, but to choose a system for creating ones that is hard to crack[13].

The approach she suggested – which is similar to those recommended by Microsoft, and other security-conscious organisations – has five steps:

1   Choose some phrases you'll remember – the first lines of favourite songs, perhaps. For example, the first line of The Password Song from 'Tigger & Pooh and a Musical Too' is: *Kaleidoscope or kindergarten, Easter Bunny, Santa Claus* which would give *'kokebsc'.*

2   Replace some of the lowercase letters with capital letters, numbers or symbols, using rules you'll find it easy to remember. You could begin and end with capitals, and replace the letters 'o' and 'e' with '%' and '3'. The end result would be *'K%k3bsC'.*

3   Customise the password for each site or application, by adding characters or numbers. To do this, decide on a system that derives the characters from the name of the website, or program, you need to access. You could choose the first two characters of the name, followed by the number of characters it contains. That would make the password for an account on BT.com *'K%k3bsCBT6'.*

4   Write down hints to remind you of the phrases and the methods you chose. Keep the piece of paper somewhere safe – in your wallet or purse, perhaps.

5   Change your passwords at regular intervals – say, every 90 days. Remember – you don't have to change everything. You could just change the phrase that's the 'root' of your

---

[13] 'A good password is a system for creating codes that are easy to remember but hard to crack', *CSO Magazine*, 15 December 2009, *http://howto.techworld.com/security/3208751/how-to-write-good-pass words.*

passwords, keeping the rules you use to substitute characters, and link passwords to sites, the same.

Technical assistance is also available in the form of a variety of password management applications. These can be used to generate strong passwords, and store them securely. You then only need to worry about remembering the single password that gives you access to the password management software.

CHAPTER 5: PEOPLE ARE HELPFUL AND TRUSTING

'You may be deceived if you trust too much, but you will live in torment if you don't trust enough.'

Frank Crane

It is natural for staff to trust people they encounter in the course of their work – especially those who are, or who seem to be, colleagues, customers or suppliers – and to try to assist them if they need help.

We are taught at our mother's knee that it is polite to hold open the door for the person following. Even if we can't see their pass, then it's probably under that jacket, or in a pocket.

But that well-dressed businessman in a hurry, tailgating his way through the security door, could well be intent on industrial espionage. And what about that group in overalls, who just arrived carrying tools and ladders? They look like members of the maintenance team, but is that who they really are? Criminals don't always wear masks and stripy jumpers, and carry bags marked 'swag'!

As Virginia socialite, Michaele Salahi, and her husband, found in November 2009, you can get access to all sorts of places if you look the part. When they turned up for a state dinner at the White House, Secret Service personnel were so convinced they were the Real McCoy, they let them in. While the couple were screened using metal detectors and so on, ' established protocols were not followed at an initial checkpoint'. (Translation: no one checked the Salahis' names were on the guest list.)[14]

Equally, it is important for people to remember that theft isn't the only problem that you are guarding your premises against. In 2005, for example, fraudsters attempted to steal an estimated £220 million from the Sumitomo Mitsui Bank, by bringing equipment into its City of London office. Dressed as cleaning

---

[14] 'White House gatecrashers met President Barack Obama', BBC News, 28 November 2009, *http://news.bbc.co.uk/1/hi/8383563.stm.*

staff, they were let in by an insider – a member of the security staff. Once inside, they connected hardware bugs to the keyboard sockets of computers used to make wire transfers. And then they left – taking nothing.

But that wasn't the end of the story. Over time, the devices transmitted keystrokes to the fraudsters' lair nearby. Gradually, the criminals learnt everything they needed to be able to transfer large sums of money into their accounts – user codes, passwords, customer account details, and so on. Fortunately, the authorities became aware of what was going on, and when wire transfers were attempted, they were blocked[15].

Even the security professionals who man IT helpdesks, find it hard to resist the pleas of damsels (and their male equivalents) in distress. When people call to say that they are working away for a few days, and need to prepare something for an important meeting, but have forgotten their password, new ones get issued, so the callers can get whatever they need.

This is an example of 'social engineering', a well-established way of getting people to divulge confidential information.

When this old-fashioned con trick is conducted via e-mail, it is known as 'phishing'. According to Internet security vendor, SonicWALL, 8.5 billion spoof e-mails were sent every month in 2008[16]. Each claimed to be from a legitimate organisation – a bank, for example – and included a very similar request: for the recipient to verify his or her username, password, and other details, by visiting a website.

Most people are wise to the problem now, which is just as well – the torrent of e-mails shows little sign of letting up. But every year, a small percentage – one report put the figure at 12.5 out of

---

[15] 'Lessons learned from biggest bank heist in history', CIO Update, 19 April 2006,
www.cioupdate.com/trends/article.php/3600126/Lessons-Learned-from -Biggest-Bank-Heist-in-History.htm.
[16] 'SonicWALL phishing and spam IQ quiz', SonicWALL,
www.sonicwall.com/phishing/.

every million[17] – mistakenly do as they are asked. They visit the fraudster's website, supply the details … and often end up paying the price. Cybercriminals were reported to have raked in £3.5 billion in 2009, by duping people. Research by Britain's Office of Fair Trading (OFT), suggests that 73% of adults received a scam e-mail in 2009, and that three million British consumers lost £3.5 billion as a result[18].

New variants on this type of attack can be extremely sophisticated, and difficult to spot. So-called 'spear phishing', is more targeted than the traditional e-mail scam, and may, for example, be aimed at the employees of a particular company. Sprinkling the e-mail with company jargon, and the names of executives and department heads, can make it highly convincing. Even more selective is 'whale phishing' (yes, I know whales are mammals, but that's what it's called), aimed at specific 'big fish', such as CEOs. Examples of whaling attacks include spoof subpoenas and tax notifications. In panic or anger at the prospect of legal action, the executive clicks on an embedded link to a realistic looking site. Those targeted may never know that, as a result, key-logging software has been installed on their PCs, to capture everything they type, including credentials, giving access to sensitive commercial information. (The heroine portrayed in Stieg Larsson's Millennium Trilogy uses the ploy very successfully[19].)

It isn't just e-mail that you have to watch either. The same basic attacks can use other channels, such as instant messaging and social networks.

It's also amazing what people will do to get a free gift. For several years, an annual experiment was conducted outside Liverpool Street station in central London. Office workers were

---

[17] 'How many people fall victim to phishing attacks?', ZDNet, 4 December 2009, *http://blogs.zdnet.com/security/?p=5084.*

[18] 'Government crackdown on cyber scams', Department for Business, Innovation and Skills, 15 January 2010, *http://webarchive.nationalarchives.gov.uk/+/http://www.bis.gov.uk/ne ws/features/2010/2/government-crackdown-on-cyber-scams.*

[19] 'The girl with the dragon tattoo' and sequels, Stieg Larsson, Quercus, 2008. First published in Sweden, 2005.

offered a chocolate bar if they participated in a survey. The questionnaire asked them for various types of personal information, including passwords, and a high proportion complied. No one tried checking the passwords, so it's possible at least some of the subjects outwitted the experimenters by giving false ones. Still, it appears that a very small incentive, offered in the right context, can be sufficient to blind people to significant risks.

Another experiment involved scattering USB memory sticks around a company campus, as if they had been dropped inadvertently. They contained an innocuous software payload, that simply sent a message back to the experimenters, when they were plugged into a PC. However, they could well have been carrying malware, with the potential to bring down the corporate network, steal information, or provide back door access to be exploited later. Again, the prospect of something for nothing made people throw caution to the wind.

To reinforce the need to beware of geeks bearing gifts, consider the case of IBM staff, who unwittingly distributed malware-infected USB drives at the AusCERT security conference in 2010. The company had to send an embarrassing e-mail to all those attending the conference: 'At the AusCERT conference this week, you may have collected a complimentary USB key from the IBM booth ... Unfortunately, we have discovered that some of these USB keys contained malware, and we suspect that all USB keys may be affected'[20]. IBM is not the first company to have done this, and will certainly not be the last.

Top tips ...

Assume nothing – make completely sure that people are exactly whom they appear, or claim, to be.

Stay alert for social engineering, spam and phishing attempts.

---

[20] 'IBM hands out malware laden USBs', IT Pro, 24 May 2010, *www.itpro.co.uk/623608/ibm-hands-out-malware-laden-usbs.*

Don't plug anything into a PC if you aren't sure where it came from.

CHAPTER 6: HARNESSING HUMAN QUALITIES TO IMPROVE SECURITY

As promised, I will now turn to look at what can be done to utilise human qualities, to improve enterprise security. Later, we will consider human factors in relation to processes and technology.

Awareness and training are fundamental. People can only help in preventing security breaches, if they are aware of the dangers, and are taught secure behaviours as part of their normal work training. An enterprise must promote a culture in which employees share the responsibility of defending the company against attack – one in which everyone knows how to behave responsibly, is alert to potential problems and understands what best to do when confronted by a potential security incident.

It is important that security training explains not only what to do, but why to do it. The reality, of course, is that effective security is a business enabler, and enhances the corporate brand – it inspires customer confidence, and has been known to help close many an important deal. The problem is that this is often not communicated, with the result that employees are aware only of the 'what', and not of the 'why'.

It is also important for people to understand the massive impact that security breaches can have on an organisation's reputation and bottom line.

One awareness campaign that has been highly praised is that of Barclays Bank. Amongst other materials, the company produced a series of videos, that are both amusing and effective. At the time of writing, several of these could be viewed on YouTube[21]. Have a look at these to see how a serious message can be delivered in an entertaining and memorable way, and recommend that your employees do likewise.

---

[21] Barclays Bank security awareness videos:
www.youtube.com/user/JonathanRhodesDotCom.

Senior teams need to know about their personal liability under international law, and the need for compliance with such legislation as the US Sarbanes Oxley (SOX) Act, that followed financial scandals involving Enron, WorldCom and Arthur Andersen. Top people sometimes view security as an overhead, and need to be persuaded that it can enhance Return on Investment (ROI), and boost the bottom line of the business. Middle managers, particularly those in sales and marketing, need to know that an effective security policy can help to close deals, as a direct spin-off of enhanced customer confidence. The general workforce should be made aware of risk, and be encouraged to 'keep the door shut', both physically and electronically. This includes everything from protecting their laptops and BlackBerrys, through to ensuring that passwords are changed regularly, and that the alarm is set by the last person to leave a building. Computer-based training is a cost-effective way of keeping people's awareness and skills up to date.

Beyond this, it is important that everyone is seen to be involved in protecting the organisation, starting again at the top. An awareness and training campaign will be undermined if executives, and senior and middle management, are not fully behind it. This needs to go beyond fine words and speeches; leaders must be seen to adopt the secure behaviours they exhort others to follow.

To quote the UK Department for Business, Enterprise and Regulatory Reform's 2008 Information Security Breaches Survey [22], 'Examples of positive behaviours showing a high-priority include IT literacy at the board level, insistence on effective back-up and access control processes, willingness to spend money, and regular engagement on security issues. Behaviours that convey a low-priority include wanting protection without being prepared to pay for it, lack of action after a security breach, poor understanding of technical issues, and too little attention to raising staff awareness'.

---

[22] '2008 Information Security Breaches Survey', Department for Business, Enterprise and Regulatory Reform, April 2008, *www.security-survey.gov.uk.*

The way managers respond to breaches is particularly important. Statistics suggest that about 80% of e-crime is caused, or enabled, by people who did not intend to do anything wrong, but did so by accident[23].

The lesson here is a simple one – if you want to keep people on your side, it is essential not to 'criminalise' anyone who simply makes a mistake. There's the danger that problems may be swept under the carpet – left to fester until they become very serious indeed. Rather, what's needed is an open and supportive environment that encourages people to 'fess up'. That way, the organisation has an opportunity to learn from its mistakes – to shut stable doors before valuable horses get the chance to bolt, or be stolen. The chance that people will report issues, will depend on their trust in the reporting scheme, which could be run by their employer, an independent agency or a government body. They will not only worry about exposing themselves to punishment and prosecution, but also about protecting their identities if they report others' failings and transgressions. The aviation industry has successfully used reporting schemes, encouraging workers to flag safety-related incidents.

Top tips ...

Train everyone in security.

Explain both 'what' and 'why'.

Run refresher courses regularly.

Security starts at the top, with the CEO. He or she must set a shining example.

Make it easy – and safe – for people to report failings ... even if it is the CEO who's at fault!

---

[23] 'Infosec: no longer just the IT department's concern', SC Magazine, May 2005,
www.scmagazineus.com/infosec-no-longer-just-the-it-departments-con cern/article/32152/.

CHAPTER 7: WHY RAISE AWARENESS?

According to the European Network and Information Security Agency (ENISA) [24] , an information security awareness programme will:

- Provide a focal point and a driving force for a range of awareness, training and educational activities related to information security, some of which might already be in place, but perhaps need to be better co-ordinated and more effective.

- Communicate important recommended guidelines, or practices, required to secure information resources.

- Provide general and specific information about information security risks and controls, to people who need to know.

- Make individuals aware of their responsibilities in relation to information security.

- Motivate individuals to adopt recommended guidelines or practices.

- Create a stronger culture of security, one with a broad understanding and commitment to information security.

- Help enhance the consistency and effectiveness of existing information security controls, and potentially stimulate the adoption of cost-effective controls.

- Help minimise the number, and extent of, information security breaches, thus reducing costs directly (e.g. data damaged by viruses), and indirectly (e.g. reduced need to investigate and resolve breaches); these are the main financial benefits of the programme.

---

[24] 'The new users' guide: How to raise information security awareness', ENISA, 1 July 2008, www.enisa.europa.eu/act/ar/deliverables/2008/new-users-guide/?searc hterm=information security programme.

BT case study

BT has developed a series of programmes aimed at prevention, education and awareness training.

Everyone in the company is required to complete a Computer-Based Training (CBT) package, every two years, and there are company-wide security clinics, and global roadshows, to keep awareness high. The company has even introduced a scheme to give financial rewards to people who have demonstrated good security behaviour.

BT also provides a 24/7 helpdesk, to provide help and advice to its employees. The helpdesk takes 20,000 calls a year from people reporting incidents, and the company is hoping to capture further reports through its intranet.

It is also important to make sure that an organisation's business processes are designed to re-enforce its security policies. For example, while the City of London Police believes only 25% of crime is reported, BT's processes force its people to do so. Whether it's a car that's damaged, or a laptop stolen, no item is replaced or repaired without a Crime Reference Number, that triggers the appropriate system.

Recently, the company distributed a booklet entitled 'BT Security: Your Part in the Big Picture', to all employees. This describes 18 desirable security behaviours. The pocket-sized format encourages staff to carry it with them in their jackets or laptop bags.

CHAPTER 8: BEYOND AWARENESS

As important as awareness campaigns and compulsory training are, they can only go so far. Training works best when it is regularly reinforced by experience, and this is a problem in the case of security. Successful security is measured by the absence of bad events, rather than the occurrence of good ones. Consequently, opportunities to reinforce positive behaviour are limited. As mentioned above, punishing staff involved in security breaches, except in cases of deliberate intent, or blatant recklessness, is not a good idea. It encourages secrecy, and gets in the way of learning, on an individual and organisational level.

For similar reasons, measuring the effectiveness of awareness and training campaigns can be difficult. But it needs to be done. It would be very easy to spend money on posters, websites and computer-based training, and complacently sit back, thinking, 'job done'. It's far better to approach the issue scientifically. First, work out what it is you are really trying to improve. Are you trying to reduce theft? Or information leakage? Or fraud? This will help focus your campaign, apart from anything else. Then find a way to quantify the problem. Establish a baseline figure, and track how this changes as the campaign progresses. Continue to measure it afterwards, as the benefits may decay as memories fade. By using a selection of different success measures, you'll avoid having too narrow a focus. You might want to review your measures periodically, as priorities, and the nature of threats your business faces, will change.

Provided the information isn't too sensitive, publishing security metrics within your organisation, can help involve staff. It aids motivation if people can feel their efforts are having some effect.

The ultimate aim should be to involve your staff, fully, in a programme of continuous improvement, that optimises enterprise performance in respect of information security. Here is a possible programme of achievement levels, presented in the manner of a capability maturity model:

- **Ad hoc:** No organised awareness or training programmes. Processes and procedures are patchy, at best.

- **Aware:** Organised campaign to make all staff aware of security issues, threats and pitfalls. Security policies are documented, and available to all employees.

- **Trained:** Job specific security procedures are established and documented, and taught as an integral part of training, for individual and team roles.

- **Educated:** Staff have an understanding of security threats and controls, and risk management techniques, that allows them to make intelligent, informed decisions, in their day-to-day work, and when exceptional circumstances arise.

- **Empowered:** People throughout the enterprise are able, and trusted, to make individual contributions to the continuous improvement of enterprise security. This could work in a similar way to the Total Quality Management programmes inspired by the writing of William Edwards Deming, that helped transform Japanese industry in the latter half of the 20th Century.

Top tips ...

Measure the effectiveness of awareness and training campaigns.

Involve staff, to drive continuous improvement.

CHAPTER 9: THE EXTENDED ENTERPRISE

'The average {large} company has US$12 million worth of sensitive information residing abroad.'

McAfee, 2009[25]

In today's complex and challenging world, few companies can do everything themselves. Most need to focus where they excel, and call on outside expertise to get other tasks done. If the outsourcing contractor needs access to sensitive or personal data, you need to consider the security awareness of its staff, as well as your own. It is important, therefore, to assess the contractor's security policies, processes and culture, as an integral part of selection procedures.

The sample security policy on outsourcing drafted by the ISO27k Implementers' Forum, makes it clear what companies should expect[26]:

5.4.3 Suitable information security awareness, training and education shall be provided to all employees and third parties working on the contract, clarifying their responsibilities relating to <ORGANISATION> information security policies, standards, procedures and guidelines (e.g. privacy policy, acceptable use policy, procedure for reporting information security incidents, etc.) and all relevant obligations defined in the contract.

Outsourcing is nothing new, of course. People have been doing it for centuries. What's different now, is that the world has gone digital, and computer data can be shipped as easily to organisations on the other side of the planet, as anywhere else. And if the organisations are in different countries, factors like

---

[25] 'Unsecured economies, protecting vital information', McAfee, 2009, *http://resources.mcafee.com/content/NAUnsecuredEconomiesReport.*
[26] 'Information security policy on outsourcing, ISO27k Implementers' Forum, 2008, *www.iso27001security.com/ISO27k_model_policy_on_outsourcing.doc*

differences in language and culture, will pose additional hazards.

This raises some interesting questions. As our world gets more interconnected, does it get more risky? Let's suppose you outsource your payroll administration to a service provider. Does the risk you face go up, or down? Does it matter where the provider is based, or does the work? Or how security conscious its staff really are?

As well as the risk of actual information disclosure, there is the possibility that you are breaking the law, just by sending the data to a different country. European legislation forbids exporting personal data to countries that do not meet the European 'adequacy' standard for privacy protection. Interestingly, the US does not qualify, due to its different legal approach to privacy. This led to the negotiation of a 'safe harbour' framework, simplifying the process by which US companies can be approved to receive data from Europe, on the basis of their internal controls.

The situation is better than it was a few years ago, when the media was full of stories about call-centre workers willing to sell customers' bank account details, and other confidential data, to criminals.

Data protection laws have been tightened, but, even today, the standards that companies in some countries apply, falls short of what would be acceptable in the UK, Europe or the US.

In April 2009, Britain's Financial Services Authority – the body that polices banks, insurance companies, and so on – said staff training in offshore call centres was ' generally poor', and urged companies to do more to make sure that staff working on their behalf were properly equipped to detect, and report, security problems[27].

---

[27] 'Poor staff vetting at offshore call centres poses crime risks', FT Adviser, 28 April 2009,
www.ftadviser.com/FTAdviser/Regulation/Regulators/FSA/News/articl

Top tips ...

Assess contractors' security policies, processes and culture, as an integral part of selection procedures.

If contractors are offshore, make sure you are entitled to send customer data to them, before you do.

CHAPTER 10: PROCESS DESIGN

'Designing-out the potential for human error leading to cybersecurity breaches, is the optimal approach to tackling the problem. If the opportunity for human error does not exist (think of automated rather than user-installed security software upgrades), then it will not occur.'

Cyber Security Knowledge Transfer Network[28]

Security is essentially about managing certain categories of operational risk, typically referred to as 'CIA' – Confidentiality, Integrity and Availability.

Standards, such as ISO27001, provide best-practice guidance in designing, setting up, operating, and improving institutions and procedures, based on risk management principles. These are known as Information Security Management Systems.

However, it is just as vital to take security into account when designing normal business processes. Security tends to be the 'Cinderella' requirement, considered belatedly as an add-on, or retrospectively, as a result of a breach or a near-miss. As a result, conflicts between security and, for example, productivity, are not recognised, let alone adequately addressed.

Human factors specialists would categorise security procedures as 'supporting tasks', rather than 'production tasks'. Production tasks are to do with the basic day-to-day value creation activity, and anything that interferes with them is noticed immediately, and addressed as a high priority. Supporting tasks generally have long-term benefit, and in the short term, can be perceived as 'getting in the way'. Security procedures that take time away from normal work, require physical effort or mental concentration, will consequently get neglected. To counter this

---

[28] 'To err is human, to design-out divine', Cyber Security Knowledge Transfer Network, 2007,
http://server.quid5.net/~koumpis/pubs/pdf/cybersecurity2007.pdf.

tendency, security must be integrated into people's tasks and business processes, rather than interfere with them.

The UK Cybersecurity Knowledge Transfer Network offers the following useful principles[29]:

Identify the performance requirements of the production task, and make sure the security task does not significantly reduce productivity.

Minimise the physical and mental workload of the security task; use a mode of interaction that fits with the production task activity (e.g. voice-based mechanisms, telephone-based interactions, or a hands-free mechanism, for tasks where both hands are occupied).

For frequently executed security mechanisms, design for speed; for infrequently used mechanisms, design for memorability (step-by-step user guidance, recognition based interfaces).

Minimise the scope for error. Human factors research, especially research studying human error, provides ample guidance on how to design systems that minimise the likelihood of error, and the impact of errors. Systems must be designed such that a single error by an individual, does not lead to serious security incidents.

Incentivise secure behaviour (as well as – or as an aspect of – productivity goals).

---

[29] 'Human vulnerabilities in security systems', Cybersecurity KTN Human Factors Working Group, 2007, *http://hornbeam.cs.ucl.ac.uk/hcs/publications/HFWG%20White%20Pa per%20final.pdf.*

CHAPTER 11: USABILITY

'A better balance has to be found between the limitations of human beings and the desire for increased security. More research on how perceptions of usability, security and convenience are related is needed.'

Hoonakker et al[30]

'Why does your computer bother you so much about security, but still isn't secure? It's because users don't have a model for security, or a simple way to keep important things safe.'

Butler Lampson[31]

Butler Lampson[32] cites two main reasons for software being insecure: bugs and conflicts. The conflicts he is referring to, are between the desire for more bells and whistles, faster time to market, lower cost and greater security. To these I would add poor usability as a distinct issue.

No matter how much you spend trying to educate people about information security, you'll face an uphill struggle if your systems and processes are hard for them to understand, or use. There are two ways of looking at the problem, that are best treated as complementary approaches, to be used in combination:

- **Don't give the user the opportunity to do bad or stupid things**: If a policy is mandatory, enforce it through automation, if possible. If decisions are too complex for the

---

[30] 'Password authentication from a human factors perspective: results of a survey among end-users', Hoonakker, Bornoe and Carayon, Proceedings of the Human Factors and Ergonomics Society 53rd Annual Meeting, October 2009, *www.hfes.org/web/Newsroom/HFES09-Hoonaker-CIS.pdf.*

[31] 'Usable security: how to get it', Butler Lampson, Communications of the ACM, vol.52, no.11, November 2009, p.25.

[32] 'Usable security: how to get it', Butler Lampson, Communications of the ACM, vol.52, no.11, November 2009, p.25.

average user, it may be better to enforce a safe (though sub-optimal) choice. Consider creating user classes, based on levels of expertise, with a wider amount of discretion given to expert users.

- **Help the user make good choices:** Where user judgement or decision making is needed, or desirable, make it as easy as possible to make the right decision. Provide an intuitive model of cause and effect, that the user can relate to. Present the information required to make the decision clearly. Explain the implications of the various options. Apply good user-interface design principles, to minimise the possibility of mistakes.

The search for design principles governing human interaction with technology, is a maturing academic and applied field of study, variously known as human factors, human-computer interaction, man-machine interface design, usability, and so on, depending on the emphasis. Some companies even have specialist labs that test usability. In general, it is something of a black art, rather than an engineering science, though in some areas, well-established principles do exist. Examples include the controls in cars, aircraft cockpit design and the now-familiar WIMP (window, icon, menu, pointing) interface on computers. These are all the result of years of co-evolution, whereby designers have responded to users' experiences, and users have learned mental models that enable them to use the controls intuitively. The result is that a driver can adapt to a new car in seconds, and a Macintosh owner can grasp the basics of the Windows® interface without instruction.

Unfortunately, we understand relatively little about what exactly it is about the way things are designed that increases – or reduces – the chance that users will accidentally do things that expose organisations to attack.

A study conducted by researchers at the University of Wisconsin-Madison, and Copenhagen's IT University, shed some light on the situation[33]. Focused on the way users select passwords, it found that security professionals are as likely to deviate from best practice, as general users. What mattered most was experience, not expertise. More advanced users were much more likely to choose 'strong' passwords, change them regularly, and so on, than novices, indicating perhaps that exposure to the consequences of security breaches increases people's desire to get everything right.

The impact of security measures in limiting users' ability to get jobs done, is something that deserves particular attention. Firewalls are an effective way to limit who can move and what, between, say, the public Internet, and an organisation's private (and hopefully more secure) intranet. However, if the restrictions they impose are too onerous, the chance that someone will merely copy files onto a memory stick, and walk around what they see as a road block, is increased. People are generally paid based on their ability to get things done, after all, not on their respect for security measures.

As the researchers at the two universities concluded, 'more research on how perceptions of usability, security and convenience are related, is needed. Perceived usefulness, ease of use and user satisfaction, determine (correct) use of technology, not the other way around'.

One approach[34] is 'to adopt a participative approach to security analysis and design – involving the stakeholders in the technical discussions and decision making, surrounding security design. Through participation, stakeholders can gain a better understanding of security issues, and become able to communicate their own security needs'.

---

[33] 'Password authentication from a human factors perspective: results of a survey among end-users', Hoonakker, Bornoe and Carayon, Proceedings of the Human Factors and Ergonomics Society 53rd Annual Meeting, October 2009, *www.hfes.org/web/Newsroom/HFES09-Hoonaker-CIS.pdf.*

[34] 'Human vulnerabilities in security systems', Cybersecurity KTN Human Factors Working Group, 2007, *http://hornbeam.cs.ucl.ac.uk/hcs/publications/HFWG%20White%20Paper%20final.pdf.*

Top tips ...

Design security software to be easy to use, as part of day-to-day work.

Better still, involve users in their design.

Don't give users the opportunity to do bad, or stupid, things.

Help users make good choices.

CHAPTER 12: AND FINALLY …

If you are responsible for the security of your organisation's information and IT systems, follow these five simple steps, to make sure members of your workforce know precisely what you expect of them:

- **Set the scene** – Make sure everyone knows why security matters to the organisation, to its customers, and to their jobs. Make it clear it's what the CEO wants them to do, and is what the CEO is doing him- or herself.

- **Train everyone** – Explain clearly, and simply, what you want people to do, and why they should do it. Reinforce the message at team level, making sure that people are applying the training in their everyday work. Put security on the standing agenda for team meetings.

- **Design security in** – Not just to your networks and applications, but into your systems, processes and culture.

- **Provide backup** – Make it easy for people to ask questions, report problems and get help.

- **Monitor, review and refresh** – Don't rest on your laurels. New threats are always emerging, people slip back into old habits and training becomes stale. Define meaningful and varied measures of security performance, assess them regularly and take early action if performance starts slipping.

EU for product safety is Stephen Evans, The Mill Enterprise Hub, Stagreenan, Drogheda, Co. Louth, A92 CD3D, Ireland. (servicecentre@itgovernance.eu)